Awakening in the Spirit

Awakening in the Spirit

JOSEPH MICHAEL SHUCRAFT

RESOURCE *Publications* • Eugene, Oregon

AWAKENING IN THE SPIRIT

Resource Publications
An Imprint of Wipf and Stock Publishers
199 W. 8th Ave., Suite 3
Eugene, OR 97401

www.wipfandstock.com

PAPERBACK ISBN: 979-8-3852-2600-9
HARDCOVER ISBN: 979-8-3852-2601-6
EBOOK ISBN: 979-8-3852-2602-3

06/25/24

This book is dedicated to two people who knew me best growing up—my brother Tony and my cousin Jeff. After they passed, I shared a poem at each of their services. May they be at peace with the Father. I want to share the one I wrote to my brother after this dedication. They were always there, whether troubled or fair; I loved them both very much. They were both brothers to me when I wrote it. I hoped it would help Tony be at peace with God.

CONTENTS

PART THREE: SPIRITUAL ATTRIBUTES

Section I

Section II

Section III

Section IV

Section V

Section VI

Section VII

Section VIII

For My Brother Tony

BROTHERS IN BLOOD AND SPIRIT

What can I say to my brother in the end?
When there is nothing left but to hold your hand,
I would rather spend the rest of my days in the same place,
Than to run and flee without you in my memory
Is there a point in this disparity?
Why do we see ourselves without a friend?
When we are on the mend,
I see an end to the sorrow,
A day that we will both laugh,
Where we will meet and reminisce
Of dreams and thoughts renewed
A new life formed in a beautiful world.
We will both see and glance, taking this new world by storm.
Not one nor two, but we all
Reunited as brothers, we are stronger.
Iron sharpening iron, an axe to behold!
Putting death to death and an end to all pain
We both share a love for family and friends.
United in blood and by blood
To pass on to the spirit renewed

INTRODUCTION

CREATION

And He Saw That It Was Good

The Earth by God was created in six days ex nihilo. In all his creation, he saw that it was good. The Spirit has been bearing itself over the waters of creation there since the beginning. You are the Spirit of Holiness abounding in the presence and have been there with those you have blessed. In their inception, Adam and Eve, the children of God, were created in blessing. Be fruitful and multiply supplied with dominion over the Earth and all that creeps upon it. We see a story of love and fruitfulness even in our fallen state. A way back to see the Spirit reunified with man. A picture of God dwelling among men.

PART ONE

The Homily of Life

SECTION I

MIGHT I INQUIRE

I am setting a scene with humble birth and meager restitution.
A man once born and filled with simple dreams of love and life.
To his folly, life slipped by, and chance torn. What should he see
but the world as it is? Where love is squandered and life wasted.
Where riches abound, power is grabbed, and the squalor of
greed. The atrocities of man were brutal and disdained. Where
is this love I seek? Does a simple act exist? Where actions do not
match reactions and happiness is bliss. Where is my lasting joy,
the monarchy of the soul? Can you resurrect my kindness? Or
will the devil snare my soul? Pray not the wily gates corrupt my
meager spirit. Please give me courage, cunning, and vigor lest my
life lie ensnared.

THE BEGGAR'S PLEA

Crazed eyes only open so far.
Dimly lit, the door fades and draws me away.
As I peer desperately into the precipice of self-reflection
Calloused and shadowed, I don my day-lit attire.
A beggar's price paid for a meager meal of mind.
Not seeing through dissolution short of peace
Cracking the barrel down a dogged path
Tripping and falling blind and barren.
Mercy bore no kindness.
Abound sweet folly of whence I would once dream.
This state would pass on to reverie.
Childish, I call it, but a memory.
Never-ending agony till the last breath cease
Waking up to the cries of all deceit
All pleasantries ended with camaraderie.
Forsaken downtrodden misery
How did I wake up to the blasphemous heresy?
Where I cry out for none to hear
It was a price paid for sanity.

ONCE ABOUT

Growing up was not so bleak.
No, surely master to shatter me.
Bonds to bedraggle nor deride my confidence.
But alas, in the end, this little bend did break.
I tore these shackles, the bonds of grey.
Abhorred no longer, I find in just stead.
New paths to travel and roads to rent.
The mischief that is not caused would be considered an ill pursuit.
Lest I cry out for the sake of truth
Why does silence reign over the night?
It is forsaken until the day of the terrors, the dismay.
One look of fright should tell, but instead, all was built up and quelled.
There is no bitter taste, and tepid water is more displeasing.
No refreshment without burdens borne.
A sacrifice made for a promise to keep.
Never to flee forever to run.
Freely about the plains

UNFILLED LOVE

Empty now but not broken.
Dredging about the sands of time
Tall crags overlooking the barren waste.
Down from here, I see from afar, but near, my lost love.
I am crushed beneath a lass so bold and full of beauty.
A death-defying leap
A never-ending plunge
Bold strokes of penned letters a renegade through the winds
My terrace is an amenity for some.
A view so quaint yet off so far
The heart beats a flickering farewell.
Tears of sundry plundered from a memory of happenstance.
As I observed this last hour, I put it to rest.
I laid my eyes on the bed and began to test.
My organs feign discontent.
It is required from a feeling of this unfilled love.

TETHERED MEMORIES

Hitched in twain brought together for a time.
Fashioned in unison, unraveled by a passing glance.
A lass of fine make who do I spy again?
I find the memories of you spinning and gleaming in my moistened mind.
Eyes of mine are altogether divine. I see the graciousness in your steps.
Saving graces of the years gone by
Counting days and hours so doubly flown
Like the majestic eagle soaring freely, bold, and trustworthy.
Spying in your mind the beauty I can only hope to imagine.
What, when, and how would it be?
The moment that you and me together will sing.
Eternal reverie of the most courageous sort
Garlands and multitudes of flowers for you, sweet babe
Oh, the mountains precious, the valleys where we were down low.
Please bring me tranquility and carry me in your arms.

SECTION II

AS I PRAY, MY SOUL IS AT EASE

To God, I pray to bring my soul to be appeased. Bring me your ever-loving mercy, tender kindness, and grace. I am down on a bent knee, not like a valiant knight—instead, a broken child with a fevered chill who needs assured remedy. In my bed at night, I cry alone for the day of break to entertain better company. Not just my lonesome self. I pray for a forest of lilies, daisies, and bright smiles from a tweeting bird—a sparrow of flight known to land in the palm of my hand. Fly by day together. We stay hand in hand from the shores of the land through the seas and storms and onto the promised lands.

CUNNING CAME THE KNIGHT

Virtutis fortitude is not lacking as I lay down.
Behold, my love is brought up with a nurturing stare.
As I wake up to face the world, suddenly, a glare.
For the end bore the fortuity of circumstance
Just a pass on by without a trapping of perchance
Where there is a cause for ill-gotten, the other did gain.
Where a thrice nobleman was cut down in vice
Where art thou fair lady?
As the breath last slips from me, passing by, serenity.
Where time from this world will tell only how we have left
Behind us all, the widow lays the gambit.
Fair lady, sweet dawning of the night
In the morning, Deadman's bells will be traded for the light.
Grave clothes, they came to rob him.
But cunning came the Knight.
The Heavenly Host descended.
Righteousness defending Truth.
The Messiah came to cut apart the widow from the dark
Reshaping her in bold fashion
Turned the widow into a bride.

PUT ASIDE YOUR SORROW

Bent, not broken upward, not down.
Passing by, I trade my eye for a candle lit in the dimmest halls.
A trill and twang from the altar came not passing without a beat.
Walking out on memories, putting aside selfish pride, barren
There is no time for vanity or selfishness, my calamity.
Heaving about this burdened body
No justice for my pleaded sanity
It is time to put aside the sorrow.
Hide all shame, pull down walls, break all ties to past fancies.
Taste of taste, I yearn for your treat, a sighting not parting nor part nor part nor pleading.
No anger I see stemming from eyes so vast and remarkable.
It was a great feeling to see, not hear, be, or bear.
Another time, I would be a sight beheld a thousand times greater than lesser.
Not a tragedy nor a calamity but a bold ender of all these travesties
From charlatans to caravanners, there is no fill for these buglers' dreams.
Pray thee I tell, for I do not see in you any more than you know what I see.
I see the bounds of love and hope that cannot be stolen.
But ever hoping a passing by and cool embrace

THE SHORES I SEE

Waters crashing waves unending tired seas of discord.
O peace be found but never a sound heard inside
This death has seen me quaking in my addled mind.
Too tired, dreary, and a malcontent
Your breeze puts me at ease and calms this ragged storm.
My mind explored and traversed a grand island of catastrophe.
Dashing a man, I thought I would be if only I could be less in pain, oh, an agony.
Fierce footsteps of a half-treaded path on the lookout, never to fall back.
A horizon dwelling among the trees of palm and shade.
No more splendor nor reason to dance.
Shadows cast like the die as I lay down tonight.
My eyes are dreary as I cry out.
Wash me away, call the curtain, curtail my memories.
Wipe it out, run the tide, and hide from me.
You see, what I am about is no end to the disparity.
So, do not run to me.
I am standing on the shores. I see.
Hiding for your sanity
Because you were the harbor for the love I need

REMEMBER OUR PARADISE

As the sand passes by and I look into the waters
I see the buoyant springs and blissful valley memories.
Of arms filled and jovial laughter alone, I reminisce.
I am passing this idle time, wondering where you are, oh dearest miss.
The one I knew or thought I did until it ended.
I thought for once how I sought and found without seeking.
But rather than as time began, parting was revealed.
Where you and I became I alone with none but less
I wake up expecting to see what was once but know this paradise is empty.
Fill me again to find my eager satisfaction.
My cup is without yearning to be filled.
I am athirst apace an aerated spring.
Without being proud but humbly seeking what is lost
Abound in my hope of hopes championing my cause.
Bear me in tranquility as I gaze upon the memories.
Where time stood still, if only for a fleeting moment
My breath caught hold, and low and beheld.
I could see below the terrace.
Waiting for your ascension

SECTION III

DO NOT DEPART MY LOVE

In your mind, I find myself longing to be. I hope I am your last thought before you slumber and wake—the decadence of peacefulness gracing your presence with tenderness. My arms would bear ten thousand burdens and then ten thousand more if only you would not leave me now nor forevermore. Captivate me with your mind's eye. Oh, the eye of mine plucks mine out, for I cannot see a lasting time without reason for you to be satisfied. Do not depart my most faithful love, for without I am more than barren. Less than the desert sands for thirst to quench and apace the driest mouth sweltering in the heat. The warmest days cannot compare to the heat from your coolest gaze. The compassion I implore you is that you lend me a borrowed ear. Hear my plea, my dearest miss. For it is this that I stand that in your presence I can scantly sit feeling I must arise unless to bow to thee humbly. My tact of tongue is scant, and formality is my lack of grace. So, read with the pen of the sword, and I will defend you faithfully.

RESTING BEAUTY

As you lay, I pray you have sweet dreams.
All your days, I will sing your praise; you are beautiful as the sun that sets.
In my greatest hopes, I sing to you a tender lullaby. That you can remember
Rock you in my arms and dance until you sleep.
You are the oxygen that fills deep within my lungs.
Bear my heart upon your shoulders and dream those sweetest dreams.
I love you like no other and see you as I should.
One thousand times or greater than the blessings for which I could hope.
Each is counted, and everyone does not fall short.
The grace of your elegance and the fairness of your countenance
You appease me in all measure the glory I see when you and I are we.
Never am I dull when I see you filled full.
You are like love lies bleeding.
I cannot wait for you to bloom.

NOT A BURDEN TO BEAR

You are not weary in my tired eyes.
As the days pass and the seasons change, your presence is stirring in my mind.
Oh, my soul quickens, and heartbeat, my arms await your sweet embrace.
I am tired of waiting but will do so forever if needed.
There is no reason to reside in my mind but to look forward to the world ahead.
There is no reason but that you lie only for my memory's sake.
The reason I say as I lay the world around me.
It is because I cannot leave without feeling sickened, without embrace.
It is a cooling gaze and sweet smile I seek.
One last chance to see what I once saw and sought.
So here I am, a once rugged man taken aback in no sudden terms.
We are brought apart by love's last shaken heart.
Into the vast unknown, I go without in tale unto woe.
Without a sign, I go by, never knowing why I try.
There is no meaning. I see what is coming and causes me to idle by
It is the dark tunnel of the cavernous cairn.
Brick by mortar, lay by hand.
Lay me down.
So, I can say that as I lay.
I see the world around me.

THE DESERT SANDS

All I bore witness to, I can no longer stand.
With no place to seek comfort
I am drier than the Negev.
For Be'er-Sheva, I thirst miles apart.
Across Jerusalem, I sit, and I weep.
Parched and weary, blind, and poor
No plea for this beggar
I sit, and I lie.
Stand, and I will die.
Without love, I am willing to embrace.
For without truth is a sacrifice I will make
No death without taste
First of the last, the greatest of the least
You come at last and cool my woe-some eyes.
Feed me my life and course through my veins.
Sustain me through your soul and comfort.

IN DEFENSE OF LOVE'S GREAT CHASM

This bliss, I miss true happiness.
Where might I once have seen this forgone thought?
Separation divine intercession I pray to reign in begged part.
Whole entrenched in an ingrained sorrow
Sort me out and bleed me tomorrow.
Pluck this tethered heart and restore.
Indwell within with peace, not sin.
Bear a fond relationship with me and her.
Where begotten unto I once was forgotten
Dropped beside the way, lulled and desperate.
Intimate, oh, I have entirely neglected this.
Song from day and flight by night
History of past mistakes gone without a trace
Future of sensations quivering about the soul
Spirits divine you, and I am inclined.
Rapport of Lovers dually one another
Seeing both eye-to-eye

SECTION IV

FAREWELL COMES IN THE DEAD OF NIGHT

I stopped, stayed, and tried to run for the last few days. Where the bleeding lies, so does my heart, which is attorned from the splitting of my chest. Dying in the hollow edge of the barren lands, my last rest avenged by the still-beating precipice. It is time to wear the attire of the memorial in reverence and respect. For as my last pardon is replete, I see the tides of change casting shadows of doubt upon a frenzied crowd. We seek the gathering of the shadows of dawn. Where do you come from? It is from the North, the South, the resolution of destitution. I seek a piecemeal, so I beg for eternal reverie. Sentenced instead, as I lie in bed today, I dread keeping the farewell promise. So, as I lay, I see this world around me, stop, and speak. Where are the last tidings of peace? Where are the sounds of the greatness of a King? When I cry out, do you hear what is needed? I see the great sound of trumpets from the seas to Galilee. Shores of water to walk upon waves of Grace that only one could be. Transplant upon my chest a new heart made of flesh. Take apart the stone, crumbling it to dust. Ashes from the fire burning out the impurities. Refiner's fire make me as you will from the desert to the promised land. There are one or more larger grains of sand. We can see a Holy façade. Only through God will there be escape: one way, one life. Jesus Christ was crucified, died, buried, and then alive. Risen arose and ascended to Glory to come back in victory.

A HEART RIPPED APART

Ragged and forlorn, disdained, and distempered
Apart for so long yet together so few
I see my heart suddenly slip.
Cut deep and pierced momentary no hold.
To have and to seek is all I require.
Lift the veil and reveal all that I seek.
Search the tide and tell me there still is a bride.
A groom for match and a heart for loom
Spin the helm and turn from the storms inside
Trouble with sanity: where did it go?
What was once a pleasant island of harmony is now a broken harbor.
Please take me to a place where there is new happiness and joy.
Where I will wake with everlasting peace
Sew back together this tattered heart.

FAREWELL'S BED

Tonight, as I die, I hope you do not stand still or cry.
As I lie in this room, a tomb is a hole in the ground.
Without walls, nothing but sands in the grain of time
This, too, lags the crags of a thousand dreams.
Or nightmares without time to tell.
Did it hurt, or did it pass? Does it stand to be judged?
Do you see, as I am the eyeless one with an addled mind?
Into the land where withers without seed
Will I rise from the ashes of death's lasting chasm?
Into the abyss I go, chains borne.
With saving strengths and bold proclamation
There is no promise of retribution outside of eternal life.
Without strife, no peace, ragged clothes of sin bore.
Tattered arms and no love left in me.
I wake up until I am at last asleep.

IN THE LAND OF GALILEE

On the mount proclaimed
Blessed be all children of God who call.
Upon the name of Jesus, listen to his mighty words.
A new heart breathed, and principles received.
Revive in me the seas' depths, the tide's running.
I wake from a thousand-year slumber with calm waves and a crashing breeze.
From out of the belly of the burdened beast, it is time to rise and awaken with Christ as a friend.
Not for a match, trouble, or worry, the tear that meets the eyes withers now dead.
It was revived in everyone, oh the calamity, the beginning, the end of tomorrow.
One shall see, and two shall be born again in the refiner's fire.
Death's last end mercy fed its previous sorrow.
Together ensured forever, we will see.
All in dignity
Peace

BORN IN CHRIST

When one dies, shall we say how to rest?
Will we seek borrowings of a past or present place or time?
Or shall we see them born again in Christ of firstborn fruits?
Labor and toil turning as the waterwheel flows.
As life's battles are strewn among us from above to below and caught between
Do we seek a new Eden and peace from the Tree of Life?
Are we the overcomers born in the resurrection?
Is the knowledge of wisdom calculated in blessings above or rooted in envy?
Is it a pity for a gambler's lot or crown of the victor found in Christ?
With no vision, we see stabbing in the dark, looking for a way.
Brighten our paths. You are the one true way.
Not a prefect without strife when given no due
Bow to the almighty; he is perfect in all ways.
The beginning and the end in all the truths

SECTION V

AS WE WAKE TOGETHER IN LOVE

The truth is that I see you as a wonderful woman to enjoy. With laughter and tears, brave the sorrows and cut back all fears. Together in body and mind-spirits entwined, we look to serve and obey with passion and praise. All we look for is love deep in the night. Together, we shall awaken in love, a sweet embrace. Yesterday's sorrows are tomorrow's homily. What we gather in this love's great light will spread in joy through peace and strength. Of God we seek together we shall breathe in the Spirit of Truth to tell the world in one accord. I dream of this, so I hope you are out there seeing this through and through. I might hope a beauty defined in God's eyes indwelt in mine. That beauty is defined by the divine, a quake causing shakes and breaking the clouds of the heavens, no rain. The sun shines, and I see the smile that puts me at ease of grace be appeased. Truth to me is that you are in the evening, the light that shines and brightens my troubled mind. As I pray for you till sleep, I ask you to be protected, at peace, in mercy, the meek, the bold, and brave for all your days. Whether together or afar, whether here or there, I do not care as long as you are safe in God's lasting embrace.

THE WONDERS OF OUR HOPE AND LOVE

To our spirits, I reply and beg and plead to God Almighty.
I hope you can become one with us and join the church.
I hope you will sing with me as I join the choir.
I can already hear your heart sing, and you make me proud.
To see you makes me glad and hope for the Spirit to indwell.
Holy Spirit of God come upon us, me and her.
So, she and I can dance in the dead of night, brightening the darkest cave.
To see what I have seen and still be loved, it would be a shame to be alone.
Forever not knowing what could have been and what ought to be.
Never thought nor heard my comforts told absurd.

SORROWS

Where we have been, you do not know.
How you have seen us is not in grace
No Godly love for us is tiring of existing for a few.
Together, we were, and now you cast afar.
Once we were close in comfort in a way
Until the time came, and we all went our ways.
You do not seek to see us together.
Only to watch us pass away.
From time to time, I stop and think.
What once was, and what I would like again.
From here to there and now a new day to begin
Can you see a new me, or am I only further down the same path?
Am I gripping onto struggles?
Or am I putting Sorrows in the past?

PRAISE GOD FOR MEMORIES

I grow tired from resting to dream of you.
Laying down in bed and seeing the best in you
What is left are pictures in my mind.
Nothing real, but in my memories of when we had been better acquainted.
No more sighs, goodbyes, or times when I laugh and cry.
Do you see me in your eyelid view?
When you rest in bed, do you pray too?
I pray with the spirit inside my life and my guide.
Humbly, I bow and say praise God today for all memories.
The days gone by, farewells aside.
Smiles and dreams are sweeter than honey and fruit.
Waking up, I wonder about dreams without slumber.
Goodbye, we say into memories you stay.

HOLY SPIRIT BE UPON YOU

With all grace and truth, I pray that you stay in grace and virtue.
I hope you will be great and see a better place in glory.
Why oh why do I not see your presence tonight in my mind?
I am conceding to reality, and that is that I am alone.
In my last prayer for you, I request.
That the spirit is upon you and all my desires are pure.

PART TWO

The Holy Spirit within Us

THE BREATH OF LIFE

Like new wineskins, pour into us the freshness of new life found only in your Spirit. Breathe into us a new creation story that fills us with your righteousness and rids us of the wages of sin and death. You left the ninety-nine to find but one, so are you the one we must see in a sea of iniquity. You are the way, the truth, and the life, and your Spirit is the only guide we need. With that Spirit, we must meditate on your word daily. Our daily bread is given to all who need it, but they should reach out and take it. Written on the heart of the believers is the Spirit of your law. In keeping with your commands, we are given new life should we have faith in you, believe, and receive your Grace. The Grace of God and the breath of life go hand in hand, following our newfound faith.

THE HEAVENS AND THE EARTH

Out of the Breath of God, the Spirit breaths life
All the light was a bore at first; that is the way and the truth.
As the Spirit cried out over the depths
All creation sang its praises back.
The sun and all other stars echo in chorus.
Perfection from your Glory entirety unified.
Undefiled and purified, a vast universe is portrayed.
All of Creation stood with purpose and intent.
For God to bless all who stand in him
Those who revere the Sacred Spirit

MAN AND WOMAN

From the dirt of the ground and bone of bones
No shame in birth nor suffering yet seen.
Perfection in their creation blessings from God
The parents of humanity
Born of a creator, the Spirit of humility
Dwelling among men living and breathing, is he?
A deeper and closer walk with the Spirit and thee
Man and women created and imparted with a blessing.
Go forth and fill the Earth with you and me.

THE FALL OF MAN

There is no greater lie than the one often repeated.
Did he say?
It was all that was needed.
With a straightforward lie, the Devil ensnared.
All of humanity for a time unknown
Through the woman first entered the sin of despair
Followed in unison by the man with death through sin.
To burden under man and pain in childbirth
To suffer and toil in the field.
To eat the dust of Earth and be defeated in the end.
A punishment just and fitting each of us.
He should strike your head, and you crush his heel.
It is a story about a savior.
One whose Spirit brings eternal light.
As well as life everlasting
But most importantly, salvation for the dead

BROKEN VESSELS

We are fallen and shattered, broken and distorted.
I am troubled by sin and death.
Rend the veil and build within us your Temple.
Make these broken vessels new and restore us with your Spirit.
We were once dry bones; send the wind upon your breath.
Breathe new life into these shallow hearts.
Write upon them the laws of your righteousness
Let the Spirit of God guide us as we meditate on your word.
The Spirit of peace upon our minds, putting us at ease

MADE NEW

In you, we are made a new creation.
Born not of flesh and blood but rather the Spirit of our Lord.
For when the flesh dies, it must be made new.
No longer flawed nor imperfect
But a beautiful picture painted by the masterful artist.
One whose brush has no false strokes.
Like a writer without flaw, his word indwells.
Through Spirit, the heart swells with joy
Not just us but the entire world that surrounds us.
This present Earth to die and be remade by his perfection.
His presence will deem us all Grace, and his Spirit imparts wisdom.

YOU ARE FLAWLESS

O Spirit above by peace of dove and wings of an eagle
You are more flawless than any fine gem.
Your peace is insurmountable and everlasting, as is your Grace.
Holiness is your chief virtue, and your serenity is unmatched.
Praise to the Holy Spirit, the one of flawlessness!
Indwelt in God and man.
For our bodies become temples to your presence
May you sanctify us and make us complete in your ways.
God almighty as a witness, we forever sing in honor and worship.
The son of God, a representative of the Lord
Come to let loose this Spirit without flaw.
That the meek may inherit the Earth, and we may seek reconciliation.

SING OF YOUR WAYS

You are the word illuminated and written upon our hearts.
To sing a song to you is like a blessed hosanna to the soul.
Holy Spirit, our guiding light, we sing to you all day.
Glory in the highest of the days
Shadows are looming no more.
Eternal reverie, our beacon of hope, the true teacher, our compass
Blessed assurance of salvation within
Searching your presence for daily life
Illuminating our garlands with whispered sonnets
Love notes from God are sacred divinity.
Peace in your sight, a strongly felt serenity.
We guard not our hearts but rather embrace them.
Your loving surrender and your glorious Grace

RENEWED IN YOU

A flesh once becoming corrupted.
Decry the unholy spirits that persecute.
Ensnare our minds and pollute.
Bring about your most Holy light.
Reign in our hearts and minds.
Renew in us the Spirit of perfection.
Deflect the fiery darts of the enemy.
Set to smolder and burn our backs with sulfur.
Rise in us, Lion of Judah.
Send the Holy Spirit in power.
The Spirit of Revival
Your tongue is flaming as a sword.
The Sword of Truth, your Holy Word
Sacred scripture God-Breathed
We are renewed in you.
It was revived in the light.
Set to illuminate the dark

BEAUTY IN MAJESTY

Holy is your Glory.
Grace is found only in your truth.
The faith in us is only found through you, Lord.
When your Spirit descends upon us and lavishes us with your seal
The divinity of the Divine is the only aspiring Majesty to which we appeal.
O Holiest of Holy's, the mightiest, the God of Israel
There is beauty in you, God of Majesty
Conqueror of souls who purifies with fire and charcoal.
Light a fire in each one of us like Isaiah
Though we do not know all the prophetic glory
Let us live in the Judgment of the Lord
For in our faith, we are found righteous through your Grace.
Burn our lips and purge our profanity.
Stop our coarse tongues and encourage our minds with your Splendor.
Set our minds heavenly and let us wander no more.
Holiest of Holy's
The Blessed Holy Spirit

GUIDING LIGHT

You have taught me all the good I know.
Taking me down the straight and narrow
No harm too great for the peace you bring.
The one excellent thing is I hope you fill the air I breathe.
With great righteousness, Majesty, and his sovereign reign
The noblest spirit of them all
Born of God the Father given as well as son
Great gifts to us to be learned in the ways of God.
So we might overcome all worries, strife, and woes.
You are our guide in all we do, showing us your character.
Ruach Hakodesh imparts upon us a seal.
Of Holiness and salvation from the King

BY GRACE WE ARE

Born of a new image in Christ Jesus
Given by the Holy Spirit that conforms us.
Praise the Grace of God that transforms us from a simple creature.
Unto the beautiful picture of flawlessness that will come
Renewal of the total sense with you in paradise
Basking in the ambiance of perpetual uniformity
Of one mind and spirit, we shall all breathe the same air in bliss.
We will all raise our glasses and never shake a fist.
No more enemies to combat nor shame, lust, or strife.
Beauty without transgression, we will see all as you do and would have.
By Your Grace, we are saved from sin, and by Your Spirit
The innermost workings of our hearts transform us.
Praise your spirit; let no ill be spoke of it.
For it is our comfort bearer and a foundation of our faith

LIKE A DOVE

Elegance and majesty ebbing like the tide.
Shining bright the likeness of no less than ten thousand stars
Of all the galaxies, not one could match what hovered.
Over the waters of creation that caused those stars to sing
A booming choir we all shall sing, sounding and resounding in Christ's name.
The Holy Spirit will inspire us to rejoice in eternal fame.
The Glory of God Almighty, his Spirit shared with us.
To envelop our minds with purity and clear our conscious mind.
Filling us with hope and drying all our tears
So, none can boast but in Christ Jesus, the savior of the Earth.
Baptized in the Jordan, the Spirit descending like a dove.
The righteous indignation of the father shows us his love.
That we may follow in footsteps and sandaled throngs
Teach us the ways of Christ.
To wash the feet and clothe the poor, we seek.
Feed and comfort those in need and nourish their very souls.

REPLACING THE SUN

Where there was once a bright ray, a beautiful beam.
Then came a rugged storm with weary waters flashing ahead.
On the boat, we sleep, hide, and cower in fear, tearing our minds.
Where is the bright ray of the sun shining upon the deck and our sails?
Please, oh God, shine upon us your creation once more for our sake
We are crashing in tumultuous sundry for the sake of our sin-bore.
What should we do to appease the God Almighty?
How can we leave our forsaken state behind?
Should we weep wherefore we are weary?
Or should we plow on through the bleak storm?
These trepidations cause us to ponder what was once but now is not.
When we first found grace but since forsake and now have fallen
For us, we come to beg and plead, come back, oh Father God
Our words you heard and sent us the song.
Whose Spirit bore and body not broken triumphed.
From a place of solace, we now pray through the trials.
Our storms are lifted in eternal reverie.
You light our paths and carry our burdens.
Dotting out the sun for the Son of God
Whom the Spirit came in recognition.
Descending upon and risen
The light upon all storms

THE GLORIOUS LIGHT OF HEAVEN

You are the source of our salvation.
The place where our strength comes from
You are the only one who can rescue us when we are weary.
You are the Great Light of Heaven
The only one who can shine so bright upon us.
Without you, there is nothing but darkness.
But in your presence, no darkness can be found.
The only joy found is in the ways of your truth.
The truth that sets us free and brings us to eternity.
With you, we will never be weary.
No empty cup borne.
No infant without a father
Nothing but your everlasting arms and peace
The dove of eternity, your Holy Spirit, reminds us of your embrace.
You are the Great Light of Heaven
No darkness can escape your grasp.
No sin can overcome you. The flawless one

PART THREE

Spiritual Attributes

SECTION I

THE BREATH OF LIFE

Used to breathe into us new life, we await the presence of your Spirit. What is dead is brought to new life, revitalized by the presence and indwelling of your most Holy Spirit. So, I seek the attributes of your character. God instilled in me the abilities of works. There are so many things to consider. Some gifts help us bear all the fruit of a mighty tree. The more of you we inhale, the more we see, act, care, and do to affect the world around us.

AIR AND WIND

Please fill me with the gift of prophecy and indulge me in the labors of the land.
Spread my wings like an eagle, mighty and rushing out of sight.
Air and winds of wisdom, your strong rushing Spirit
It makes us workers in the light of truth.
As we bring words of wisdom to the seas of trial and circumstance
Come bearing your powerful breath that renders all evil void.
In your presence, our air is sustained and raised in righteousness.
Lord, make me a miracle that will let the world know.
Of the love you have shown for me and shared with me
The connection is growing deeper day by day.
I can see you showing me the secrets of your Holy ways.
You take away all my fears and wipe out all my tears.
Please seal me with your Holy Spirit.

SECTION II

YOUR ANOINTING LORD

We see a more outstanding picture of prosperity as we abide in you and you in us. Your anointing is not a simple emotion but an inescapable calling to a higher means of servitude. The knowledge that shaped the prophets speaks to us through your Spirit. Help us be teachers and speakers of what is wise so that we can help those who need to see through blinded eyes. It is the time for us to open the eyes of everyone and evangelize the impoverished souls of man.

POUR ME THE OIL

Baptize me in your Holy Spirit, Lord, send it to me in kind.
Pour the sacred oil upon me and call upon me as your son.
Anoint me as a shepherd, and I will tend to the flock with care.
Preaching good words to both wise and poor, rich and weak, and the very meek
Keep me humble in your presence and respectful of the calling.
How do I understand without indeed I do not
You are the helper and comforter when I have not.
Do with me as you will, as I only wish to serve.
I want to be a worker for you, so do your mighty work through me.
I and I make me alone, so bring into me your presence so we can become one.
Not sensually, but in a spiritual endeavor to liven up with hope.
Please help me get the Spirit's truths so others can be free.
Bringing heaven nearer to earth

SECTION III

GREAT COMFORTER

Comfort me in the darkest times; your Spirit helps me obey. Even on the most challenging days, I will laugh and cry, seeking your ways. Oh, great Spirit of the Lord, you teach me to obey, stay up late, and pray. I would love to receive great love, fondness, and compassion for my struggles. You are the strength in my weakness, the light of my path, and the bearer of my iniquities. Please help me to be like you and be a light, too. The world may see, brighten with glee, and listen to the Lord.

COMFORT IN TRIALS

You are our great love in our trying times.
The breath of life when all else dies.
You are the peace among the chaos.
The comfort in all these trials
I seek your guidance when I am weary.
Your strength when all grows bleary.
You send others there to pray for me in kindness.
You bring the light to the darkest caves.
The one proper way to joy and happiness that I crave.
In all your ways, I seek the depths of your fantastic comfort.
Depths are tremendous and vast, like the arms that shed blood on the Cross.
The arms that healed so the Spirit to us can yield.
Fruits so unique and broad in comfort and joy

SECTION IV

HOLY WIND AND FIRE

Oh, Holy Pentecost, where first the wind met spirit fire. By your decree, you entered us and filled us with your power. By your power, we go forth decreeing in your name. Mighty tongues filled with truth spread the Gospel everywhere. Healing winds and God's holy fire are spreading to spare our sins and despair. Send the wind to spread and fan the flame as we proclaim the Holy name of Jesus Christ, the one true King—Messiah our God, your never-ending reign. Fill us with your meditated words and brighten us with that Holy wind and fire.

PENTECOSTAL FIRE

The time is now to prophesy, oh sons and daughters of the King.
It is time for the visions and dreams of young and old.
It was foretold by Peter so bold in a sermon so long ago.
Pour out your spirit, Lord, on all your servants that we may do your earnest work.
For Christ was crucified by man who defied and taunted with the cross
Our souls were not abandoned to Hades nor the Holy One to see corruption.
The Holy One Christ, messiah, the son of David
Cut to every heart with the sword so sharp.
Bringing light to a darkened world
That Wind and Fire we so desire from God, so brave and bold
From Galileans to Gentiles, bring the gospel everywhere.
Reinstate in us the fire and flame. Bring upon us your Holy name.
Jesus Christ the risen King

SECTION V

DOVE OF PEACE

You are the superb Dove of Peace from the boat after every storm. You are the fill we see when two doves nestle together in harmony. White and pure with Holiness assured. As John baptized Jesus, who had no sins, he did arise and would save the world with selfless acts, grace, and tact. He who will purge sin from the Earth. Land upon us, oh Holy Dove of Peace, with all grace upon a nest in a tree. Bear us as your Spirit's child and rear us in your ways—no bird of prey but one of love, kindness, patience, giving boundless joy to all.

ON HOLY WINGS

Soaring above with wings greater than any angel
Peaceful breeze blowing, signaling the Dove's soft landing.
Envelop me with your spirit; encompass me with your holy wings.
Bring within me your sinless ways and impart upon me the rest of the days.
A cooling breeze, this dove of peace with wondrous gaze
Seeing all there is to see and knowing all we plead, you teach us.
Make our hearts a nesting place where the spirit can breed and spread.
Like the dove with sweet surrender and tranquility
Joy, laughter, and friendship pass from one to the other in earnest.
These holy wings cause us all to stand and sing a great song of praise.
Oh, Holy Lord, guide us with your Holy Spirit
Prince of Peace is our guide. It is in his ways we meditate.
He is waiting for His Spirit to pass on to us.
That we may love one another happily.

SECTION VI

OUR INTERCESSOR

Provider of the peace you bring upon us even in the dark. When all else seems lost, you are there in our stead. As Christ bore the cross and the blood he shed. So does the Spirit intercede as each we groan out to God. The more the symphony, the more we plead, the greater our God, even our agony. To God be all glory, with the Holy Spirit filling us full of strength and peace through hardship. A peace that passes all understanding and causes this suffering to be a noble task. For with him, we are one with the way, the truth, and the light.

GROANINGS OF CREATION

We are all created crying for our master.
Please come for us and fill us with your eternal guidance.
Set our paths straight and narrow so that we might find you in the end.
We seek in you not an end to pain but an end to sin and death thereof.
Fill us with life, oh healer, intercede for us in pain.
Bring us into your glory, or help us to spread it everywhere.
Like good disciples, spare us not the rod. Please show us your ways
Wonderful God and Shepherd, your spirit is imparted to us.
That we might not delay in our journey to and abroad
Wherever we go, we all know no matter the cost you have bought.
All with your cleansing blood of sacred spotless Lamb
The spirit breathes and puts us at ease.
The groanings of your creation

SECTION VII

FRUITS OF THE SPIRIT

You bring us love, joy, peace, patience, kindness, goodness, faithfulness, gentleness, and self-control. Bear in us these fruits from the tree of spirituality eternal. Make us a mighty fig tree with plenty to share. To feed one another and to reap and sow without any tares. Remember that all can be what they should be with you. But without, we are as though dead. Cut out of us our bitter roots to keep our tree mighty and strong. Water the grove and watch us grow in boldness.

FRUIT BEARING

Our love for one another comes first from your love for us.
Joy comes in your presence and spreads when you dwell in us.
Patience from your loving arms teaches us how to operate according to your timing.
Kindness is shown by following your example of how to treat each other.
Goodness is bearing fruit and sharing it with all.
Faithfulness is delivering the truth no matter what.
Gentleness is being kind in all circumstances and to all people.
Self-control teaches us to be tempered in our actions.
These are the fruits born of your humble spirit.

SECTION VIII

THE HOLY SPIRIT AND POWER

As a part of the Godhead, we see all power in your Omnipotent Holy Spirit. There is nowhere that your grace ever fails us, and we always endure with you there. When the Holy Spirit comes upon us, it is with the power that could make a grown man fall to his knees. The power of that spirit dwells within us in the very air we breathe. It fills us with the whole measure and makes us all we have come to be. It changes every sinner it consumes into a beacon of light for God.

SPIRIT OF POWER

Send out your power of love, oh God, bring to us your might!
Dwell within your people and make them a devout nation.
The spirit of power that strikes you where you stand.
Makes moves unshakable, shatters walls unbreakable.
As we march around the cities, please give us the power like Israel at Jericho.
Trumpets blaring truth of God, let nothing else depart from these lips.
God is with us in the fires of Babylon.
No false idols hold power to match your spirit.
Put to these lips the charcoal to cleanse and speak your words of truth.
The power of your prophetic word guides our paths to you.
We see no error when brought up in your wisdom.
It is the power of that love that is unshakable.
The joy that is unspeakable causes even the boastful to be silent
Let it be to boast in the greatness of the powers of God's ways.
The power of God stands louder than any thunderclap.
More pealing lightning than any storm seen.

CONCLUDING VERSES

Proverbs 31:10–12

"A wife of noble character who can find? She is worth far more than rubies. Her husband has full confidence in her and lacks nothing of value. She brings him good, not harm, all the days of her life."

Proverbs 11:13–17

"A gossip betrays a confidence, but a trustworthy person keeps a secret. For lack of guidance a nation falls, but victory is won through many advisers. Whoever puts up security for a stranger will surely suffer, but whoever refuses to shake hands in pledge is safe. A kindhearted woman gains honor, but ruthless men gain only wealth. Those who are kind benefit themselves."

1 Corinthians 3:13–17

"Their work will be shown for what it is, because the Day will bring it to light. It will be revealed with fire, and the fire will test the quality of each person's work. If what has been built survives, the builder will receive a reward. If it is burned up, the builder will suffer loss but yet will be saved—even though only as one escaping through the flames. Don't you know that you yourselves are God's temple and that God's Spirit dwells in your midst? If anyone destroys God's temple, God will destroy that person; for God's temple is sacred, and you together are that temple."

Revelation 21:1–7

"Then I saw 'a new heaven and a new earth,' for the first heaven and the first earth had passed away, and there was no longer any sea. I saw the Holy City, the new Jerusalem, coming down out of heaven from God, prepared as a bride beautifully dressed for her husband. And I heard a loud voice from the throne saying, 'Look! God's dwelling place is now among the people, and he will dwell with them. They will be his people, and God himself will be with them and be their God. "He will wipe every tear from their eyes. There will be no more death" or mourning or crying or pain, for the old order of things has passed away.' He who was seated on the throne said, 'I am making everything new!' Then he said, 'Write this down, for these words are trustworthy and true.' He said to me: 'It is done. I am the Alpha and the Omega, the Beginning and the End. To the thirsty I will give water without cost from the spring of the water of life. Those who are victorious will inherit all this, and I will be their God and they will be my children.'"

CONCLUSION

True Prosperity in Christ
John 6:32–35

"Jesus said to them, 'Very truly I tell you, it is not Moses who has given you the bread from heaven, but it is my Father who gives you the true bread from heaven. For the bread of God is the bread that comes down from heaven and gives life to the world.' 'Sir,' they said, 'always give us this bread.' Then Jesus declared, 'I am the bread of life. Whoever comes to me will never go hungry, and whoever believes in me will never be thirsty.'"

True faith in Jesus Christ, the bread from heaven, is not simply acceptance or allowance into your life. It is total submission to and faith in God the Father through the Son through the Holy Spirit. The only way repentance can come to sinners such as us is to receive the Gospel message—not in part but in the whole. The Gospel is not filled with simple salvation but rather a total message, a complete calling. But a calling to what?

We Are All Sinners
Romans 3:21–26

"But now apart from the law the righteousness of God has been made known, to which the Law and the Prophets testify. This righteousness is given through faith in Jesus Christ to all who believe. There is no difference between Jew and Gentile, for all have sinned and fall short of the glory of God, and all are justified freely by his grace through the redemption that came by Christ Jesus. God presented Christ as a sacrifice of atonement, through the shedding of his blood—to be received by faith. He did this to demonstrate his righteousness, because in his forbearance he had left the sins committed beforehand unpunished—he did it to demonstrate his righteousness at the present time, so as to be just and the one who justifies those who have faith in Jesus."

We all have sinned, no matter how big or small it may seem. We are saved by faith in Jesus Christ through his Grace. The blood of Christ was shed on the cross as a perfect sacrifice that fulfilled the law and prophets. Submission to God is not simply to the law but to his Spirit, Authority, and Will. His Spirit lives in all who believe in him and have received the gift of eternal life. His authority is found in his dominion as the Creator and Lord of all things. Finally, his will is found in his word and prayer. The Bible gives the foundational principles for living godly; prayer allows communication with God.

Deserving of Damnation but Freed to Everlasting Life
Romans 6:17–23

"But thanks be to God that, though you used to be slaves to sin, you have come to obey from your heart the pattern of teaching that has now claimed your allegiance. You have been set free from sin and have become slaves to righteousness. I am using an example from everyday life because of your human limitations. Just as you used to offer yourselves as slaves to impurity and to ever-increasing wickedness, so now offer yourselves as slaves to righteousness leading to holiness. When you were slaves to sin, you were free from the control of righteousness. What benefit did you reap at that time from the things you are now ashamed of? Those things result in death! But now that you have been set free from sin and have become slaves of God, the benefit you reap leads to holiness, and the result is eternal life. For the wages of sin is death, but the gift of God is eternal life in Christ Jesus our Lord."

Death is not the end of existence. There is such a thing as the second death. It is where we are not merely separated from God but tormented for our rebellion. For obedience to sin makes you a slave to death. For the truth of God sets you free from death; believe in Christ Jesus. We believe in his death on the cross, burial, and resurrection from the dead to ascend to heaven and be at the Father's right hand.